D0899183

MAYFLOWER FAMILIES
Through
Five Generations

DESCENDANTS OF THE PILGRIMS
WHO LANDED AT
PLYMOUTH, MASS. DECEMBER 1620

VOLUME SEVEN

SECOND EDITION

FAMILY
PETER BROWN — *Robert S. Wakefield, F.A.S.G.*

Published by
General Society of Mayflower Descendants
2002

Second Printing, 2002

Library of Congress Cataloging-in-Publication Data (Revised for Volume 21)

Mayflower Families Through Five Generations

Edited by L. M. Kellogg and others. Includes bibliographical references and indexes

Contents:

v.4. Family: Edward Fuller, by Bruce Campbell MacGunnigle, CG
v.5. Families: Edward Winslow, by Ruth C. McGuyre & Robert S. Wakefield
                  John Billington by Harriet W. Hodge
v.6. Family: Stephen Hopkins by John D. Austin
v.7. Family   Peter Brown by Robert S. Wakefield, FASG
v.8. Family   Degory Priest by E. Townsend, R.S. Wakefield, FASG & M.H. Stover, CG
v.9. Family   Francis Eaton by L.D. Van Antwerp, MD, CG & R.S. Wakefield, FASG
v.10. Family   S. Fuller by R.S. Wakefield, FASG
v.11. Family   Edward Doty by Peter B. Hill (3 Volumes)
v.12. Family   Francis Cook by Ralph Van Wood, Jr.
v.13. Family   William White by Robert M. Sherman, FASG & Ruth W. Sherman,FASG,
                  Robert S. Wakefield, FASG
v.14. Family   Myles Standish by Russell L. Warner & Robert S. Wakefield, FASG
v.15. Families   James Chilton by Robert M. Sherman, FASG & Verlo Delano Vincent,
                  revised by Robert S. Wakefield, FASG
                  Richard More by Robert M. Sherman, FASG, Robert S. Wakefield,
                  FASG, & Lydia Dowfinlay
v.16 Family   John Alden by Esther Littleford Woodworth-Barnes & Alicia Crane
                  Williams (2 Volumes)
v.17 Family   Isaac Allerton by Robert S. Wakefield, FASG & Margaret Harris Stover, CG
v.18 Family   Richard Warren by Robert S. Wakefield, FASG (3 Volumes)
v.19 Family   Thomas Rogers by Alice Westgate, revised by Ann T. Reeves
v.20 Family   Henry Samson by Robert M. Sherman, FASG, Ruth W. Sherman, FASG &
                  Robert S. Wakefield, FASG
v.21 Family   John Billington by Harriet W. Hodge revised by Robert S. Wakefield, FASG

1. Pilgrims (New Plymouth Colony): Genealogy
    2. Massachusetts: Genealogy
        I. Kellogg, Lucy Mary
        II General Society of Mayflower Descendants

F63 M39   929' .2'0973   75-30145

ISBN No.   0-930270-06-1

HISTORY OF THE FIVE GENERATIONS PROJECT OF THE GENERAL SOCIETY OF MAYFLOWER DESCENDANTS

The concept of this genealogical project was first formally conceived by Herbert Folger in San Francisco and George E. Bowman in Boston around the turn of the century. The format was a version of the Alden Memorial published in 1867. The project officially began when it was approved at the annual meeting of the General Board of the Society on September 11, 1959.

In the first twenty-one years of the project there were three volumes of genealogies published entitled "Mayflower Families Through Five Generations". The families of seven Mayflower passengers are included in these genealogies.

Since 1990 many volumes have been added to the series. Many of the early volumes have been rewritten to bring them up to current day standards. In addition, second updated editions have been published for some families.

The Society is also publishing a series of booklets called "Mayflower Families in Progress" (MFIP), which contain four or five generations of the families we have yet to publish in the hard cover format. These genealogies contain all the information we currently have while further research continues.

The goal of the Project is to provide documentation from primary sources for all data contained in our genealogies. Our aim is to make this material available to the general public and in doing this work we are fulfilling the objects of our Society.

Edith Bates Thomas, Director of the Five Generations Project

THE SOCIETY EXPRESSES THANKS

The Mayflower Society is grateful to many people for assistance in preparing this volume for publication. Some names have unfortunately escaped the record, but the contribution of each is appreciated and herewith acknowledged.

The Mayflower Society wishes to thank Ann T. Reeves, Robert M. Sherman, Ruth Wilder Sherman, and Neil D. Thompson for their major contributions to this manuscript.

The Society also thanks Robert C. Anderson, Esther Littleford Woodworth-Barnes, Loring T. Briggs, Natalie S. Butler, Charles W. Farnham, Jane Fletcher Fiske, George P. Howard, Roger D. Joslyn, Duncan M. MacIntyre, Barbara L. Merrick, Stanley E. Moore, Bette C. Mott, Carol Roberson, H. L. Peter Rounds, Morton W. Saunders, Ethel Farrington Smith, Margaret H. Stover, Mrs. Ellis A. Waring, Alicia C. Williams, Ann S. Lainhart, and Ralph Van Wood Jr. for their contributions to the Peter Brown Family.

Five G. Chairmen: Robert M. Sherman, Cathryn P. Lanham, and Edith Bates Thomas.

INDEX: Roger D. Joslyn and Jane Fletcher Fiske

PREVIEWED BY: Ann S. Lainhart

TYPING: Cay Lanham

PREPARING CAMERA-READY COPY: Ann S. Lainhart

iv

OFFICERS OF THE GENERAL SOCIETY

1999 - 2002

GOVERNOR GENERAL	Mr. Eugene A. Fortine
ASSISTANT GOVERNOR GENERAL	Col. William T. Lincoln
SECRETARY GENERAL	Mrs. Carol Smith Leavitt
TREASURER GENERAL	Mr. Marlin W. Brossart
HISTORIAN GENERAL	Mrs. Caroline Lewis Kardell
ELDER GENERAL	The Reverend John H. Case
CAPTAIN GENERAL	Mr. Robert E. Davis
SURGEON GENERAL	Dr. Dennis E. Ward, MD
COUNSELLOR GENERAL	Ms. Asenath M. Kepler

EXECUTIVE COMMITTEE MEMBERS-AT-LARGE

Mrs. Edith Thomas   Mrs. Mary Ellen Byrne
Mrs. Patricia King Davis

FIVE GENERATIONS PROJECT COMMITTEE

2002

Director, Mrs. Edith Bates Thomas
Col. Robert Allen Greene
Mrs. Caroline Lewis Kardell
Mrs. Frank W. Lanham
Mr. Robert S. Wakefield

TO THE READER

No five-generation genealogy is ever complete. The author has assembled the family as correctly and as completely as circumstances permitted. The work is based largely on carefully researched articles in genealogical journals and family histories, together with probate and land records, and town and church vital statistics. Family tradition, in the absence of confirmatory evidence, has not been accepted as proof of a line. This has, regretfully, resulted in the rejection of a few lines which the society accepted in its early years, but were based on insufficient or erroneous evidence. On the other hand, many new potential lines have been uncovered.

Paucity of records sometimes renders it virtually impossible to follow a family or individual to another town: An entire family disappears, or one or more children are labelled "n.f.r." (no further record found). The author often offers tentative identifications using the word probably, when evidence is nearly conclusive, and possibly, when evidence is merely suggestive. This is done in the hope that a reader, tracing back his ancestry through such clues, may come upon real proof and so establish the new line.

Spelling was far from consistent even after the Revolution. To a great extent names in this book have been spelled as found in each record. This often provides different spellings of an individual's name at his birth, upon marriage, and in a deed or will. For example, Hayward is found as Heywood and even Howard for the same person; Marcy and Mercy are many times interchangeable. With variant spellings so commonplace, use of "[sic]" is restricted to exceptional examples. To assist the reader, most variant spellings of a name are lumped together in the Index, rather than separately alphabetized.